Through the Eyes of John

THE BELOVED APOSTLE WATCHES THE SAVIOR'S FINAL DAYS ON THE EARTH

ISBN: 1-932898-16-6
e. 1

Published by:
Spring Creek Book Company
www.springcreekbooks.com

Cover design © 2004 Spring Creek Book Company
Cover and Interior design by Nicole Cunningham

Printed in Korea

My name is John. I am a special witness of Jesus Christ.

Jesus called me to be one of his apostles when he began his ministry, and for three years I walked and talked with him. I also defended him before the people of Jerusalem, and mourned with him when those people rejected his message. Yet I never truly understood Jesus and his mission until those final, painful days of his life.

During that week I watched my dearest friend transform from being not only a powerful teacher and healer, but also become the Savior of the World. I was a part of those miraculous final days, and I now share them with you.

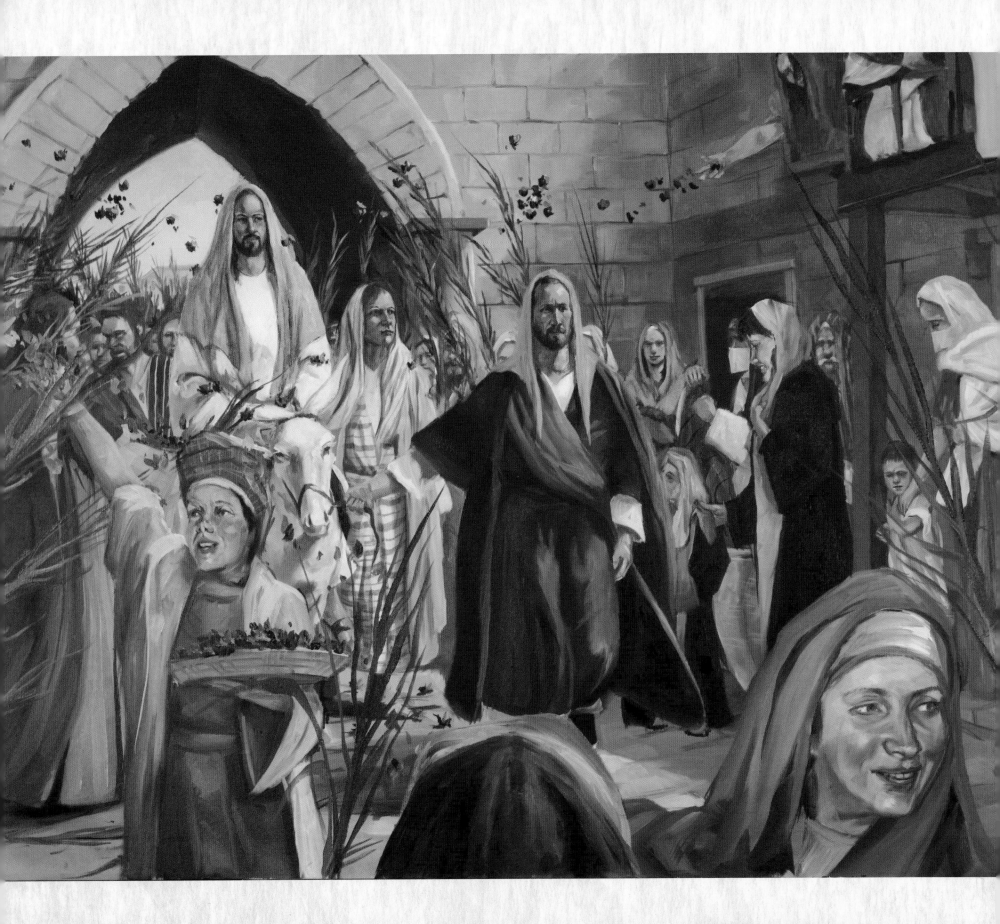

That terrible yet glorious week began as we traveled to Jerusalem for the Feast of the Passover. The people heard of Jesus' arrival, and they took branches of palm trees and went forth to meet him. They shouted, "Hosanna, blessed is the King of Israel that cometh in the name of the Lord."

Jesus rode on a young donkey, slowly and peacefully making his way to the great city. The people spoke of the miracles he had performed, such as raising Lazarus from the dead. I watched this great procession with joy.

Yet I also knew that the Pharisees were not pleased with Jesus. They feared his popularity among the people. I sensed trouble lay ahead.

John 12:12-19

We journeyed to the outer courts of the temple, where many people wanted to meet Jesus.

We sat on the steps and Jesus answered their questions. At one point, he said, "The hour is come, that the Son of man should be glorified." I didn't fully understand what Jesus meant, but I knew that Jesus was feeling troubled. In a sorrowful tone he prayed, "Father, glorify thy name."

Jesus and I stepped among the large pillars of the temple. While we talked, a deep rumble was heard by the people. Some said it was the crack of thunder, while others felt it was the voice of an angel. I heard it plainly. The Father had responded to his beloved son, saying, "I have both glorified it and will glorify it again."

John 12:20-30

The Savior's final week continued with a special supper with his twelve apostles. I was privileged to sit beside Jesus. He still carried a feeling of sadness. This was new to me. I had always known Jesus to be quick to smile, but I sensed he was carrying a heavy burden, and I watched him closely, hoping to be able to help him if possible.

We were troubled when Jesus sent away the apostle Judas Iscariot, telling him, "That thou doest, do quickly."

Then Jesus lifted us through his words of love. Jesus told us, "A new commandment I give unto you, that ye love one another. As I have loved you, that ye also love one another. By this shall all men know that ye are my disciples, if ye have love one to another."

During his time of agony, Jesus was thinking of us.

John 13:23-35

ollowing our supper, Jesus asked the apostles Peter, James and myself to join him in a nearby garden to pray. Night had fallen, and we felt very weary after our long day. Jesus asked us to keep watch near the garden's gate. Jesus then went into the garden, known by the name Gethsemane. I saw him kneel in prayer, then slump down as if in agony. I was concerned, but I noticed Peter and James had drifted off to sleep. Against my best efforts, I did also. My next recollection is seeing the Savior standing above us, his face filled with frustration. He asked us, "Why sleep ye? Rise and pray, lest ye enter into temptation."

I now know that Jesus was suffering that night for the sins of the world, yet I was unable to stay awake for him.

Luke 22:45-46

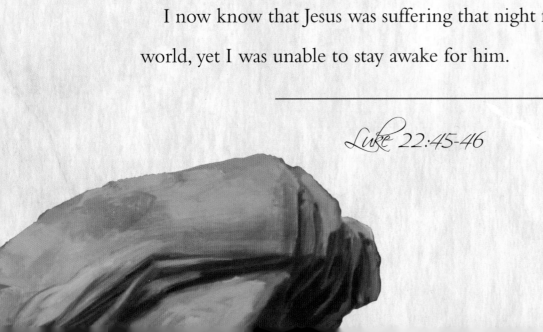

When we finally emerged with Jesus from the Garden of Gethsemane, he looked emotionally spent. I supposed we would now find a place to sleep the rest of the night, but outside the garden's gate I saw a group of men awaiting us. They carried torches and weapons. Jesus stepped toward them and asked, "Whom seek ye?"

One of the men responded, "Jesus of Nazareth."

Jesus then said, "I am he."

The group fell backward and to the ground. I saw our fellow apostle Judas Iscariot approach Jesus and kiss him on the cheek. I sensed it was an act of betrayal.

Jesus told the group, "If ye seek me, let these go their way." He then pointed to us and beckoned for us to leave him. But we would never consider such a thing.

Peter, always the impulsive one, took his sword and cut off the ear of the high priest's servant. Jesus was not pleased with Peter's actions, and he picked up the ear from the ground and healed the man. Then the officers took Jesus and bound him with ropes, although he had never given any hint that he wouldn't go with them.

Peter, James and I watched in stunned silence. Our Master was being led away like a common criminal.

John 18:1-13

eter, James and I went our separate ways, each feeling confused at what was happening. I chose to follow behind the group that held Jesus captive. They eventually led Jesus before Pilate, the Roman governor. I desperately wanted to be by Jesus' side as I had been at the supper earlier that evening, but I was restrained by the Roman soldiers. I could only watch from a distance as my heavenly king faced questions from a worldly ruler.

Pilate asked Jesus, "Art thou a king then?"

Jesus answered, "Thou sayest that I am a king. To this end was I born, and for this cause came I into the world, that I should bear witness unto the truth."

My heart was breaking to see Jesus treated this way.

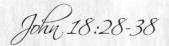

John 18:28-38

To my dismay, Jesus was taken away to a dungeon to be scourged and smitten. He suffered the painful, humiliating lashes from the whips of the Roman soldiers, who mocked him and spit upon him. Then one soldier made a crown of thorns and put it on Jesus' head, sinking the thorns deep into the Savior's skin. My mind was reeling, not quite able to believe what I was seeing. My dearest friend was being treated cruelly and unjustly, and I could only watch, helpless to do anything about it.

John 19:1-6

That horrible night soon turned to day, and I helped the other apostles gather together Jesus' followers. My heart was filled with grief and as we received word that Jesus would soon be crucified. I led Jesus' mother Mary to Golgotha, where Jesus had been nailed to a wooden cross between two thieves. We watched in disgust as the Roman soldiers cast lots on who among them would keep Jesus' clothing. We stayed near Jesus throughout the day, and I assured Jesus I would take his mother into my home. Then Jesus, the Savior of the World, died. The pain of that day is still almost too much to bear.

John 19:17-34

$\mathcal{I}$ stayed with and comforted the women as our beloved friend, Joseph of Arimathaea, arranged with Pilate so that he could take away Jesus' body and give it a proper burial. Nicodemus also came, and the two men placed the body in linen clothes and carried it into a new tomb that had never been used. We covered the opening with a stone, then I escorted the women home. Soon I fell into a troubled sleep, unable to comprehend what had happened to my Savior. My entire world had collapsed around me, and it felt as if there was little left to hope for in this life.

John 19:38-42

For the next two days, the Savior's followers stayed together, hidden from the world. We were unsure how to begin to rebuild our lives. For the past three years we had devoted ourselves to the Savior's mission and teachings, and now he was gone.

Then early on the morning of the third day after Jesus' death, Mary Magdalene came to us, saying someone had rolled the stone away from the opening of the tomb. Both Peter and I were angry that such a thing could have happened, and we both ran to the tomb. I was the first one there, and I looked in and saw Jesus' burial clothes lying there. Peter quickly rushed past me into the tomb and I joined him inside. We stared at the burial clothes, puzzled and upset that someone would take away the Savior's body. Little did we know that a marvelous event had taken place that would change the future of the world.

John 20:1-10

After seeing the empty tomb, our spirits were very low. We finally decided that it was time to return to our labors as fishermen, which we had done before heeding Jesus' call into the ministry. We boarded our fishing boats and spent the night on the sea. We caught nothing during that miserable night.

As the sun rose the following morning, we saw a man standing on the shore. He asked us if we had caught any fish. We told him no, and he said, "Cast the net on the right side of the ship, and ye shall find." We did as the man said, and to our surprise our nets were filled with so many fish that we couldn't lift the nets.

Then like a thunderbolt it hit me who was standing on the shore. I said to Peter, "It is the Lord." The ever impulsive Peter jumped into the sea and swam to the Savior, while the rest of us hurriedly steered our boats to shore.

What a wonderful reunion it was! My heart was filled with joy and love as I reached him and reverently felt the marks in his hands and feet. The Son of God lived!

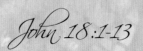

John 18:1-13

For the next forty days, the Savior stayed with us, teaching us the gospel message that we would share with the world. Then the Savior departed, promising to return again in great glory. Many years later, as I was imprisoned for the gospel's sake on the isle of Patmos, I was given a vision of that glorious day. He will come in clouds of glory, and every eye shall see him. It will be a great day for the righteous, and a dreadful day for the wicked. I testify that his return will be soon, and I also testify I have seen the resurrected Savior with my own eyes. Jesus Christ lives and will come again!

Revelation 1:7,9

ARTIST'S COMMENTARY

THE SAVIOR ARRIVES TRIUMPHANTLY IN JERUSALEM

The painting is designed to show the Savior entering through the gate into a poorer section of Jerusalem, His arrival is greeted with shouts of joy, bringing people out of the buildings to see the cause of the noise. The women are spreading the word, saying, "Here comes Jesus, here comes our king." The boy throwing the flowers symbolizes the joy Christ brings. Peter and John, however, are feeling more cautious, acting almost like bodyguards or protectors. The children in the painting are either celebrating or being held back from rushing to the Savior. The Savior's face carries a solemn look of calm satisfaction as he enters the final week of his life.

JESUS AND JOHN HEAR THE FATHER'S VOICE

At the temple, I wanted something more personal. Here the Savior has pulled John aside, among the huge columns of the temple. The painting emphasizes that John and Jesus have a special connection. John wasn't just an acquaintance of Jesus, he *knew* Jesus. Then they hear a deep rumbling. While others hear thunder, Jesus and John hear the voice of God. You'll note that throughout the book, John is wearing the same clothing, as he likely did throughout this time period. The blue and white stripes were used to let him stand out and be identifiable in each painting.

CHRIST INSTITUTES THE SACRAMENT

This is one of my favorite paintings. This again shows the special affection John has for the Savior. John can sense the heaviness and inner torment that has settled upon Jesus. The arms of other apostles are visible, but their faces aren't seen, because I wanted to focus on this key relationship. In this scene, Jesus is mentally gathering himself before teaching the apostles about the Sacrament and to love one another. Jesus' eyes are focused to his left, which symbolizes looking to the future. The bread and wine are also placed on his left side, symbolizing the upcoming fulfillment of the Law of Moses and the introduction of the Law of the Gospel.

CHRIST APPROACHES HIS SLEEPING APOSTLES

As the Savior approaches his sleeping apostles, the disappointment is evident in his face. At this crucial time when the weight of the world is on his shoulders, he was hoping his apostles could at least stay awake. In this scene, it is apparent that Peter and James are in deep sleep, while John's posture reflects that he has been awake and watchful, but just happens to be resting his eyes for a moment when the Savior approaches. I have seen another painting of this moment where the apostles' faces are turned away from Christ. I didn't want to do it that way, because even though the apostles are asleep, they are looking toward Christ. The background doesn't include Jerusalem, symbolizing how the Savior's experience in the Garden of Gethsemane leads mankind to spiritual freedom, away from worldly desires and ambitions.

JUDAS BETRAYS THE SAVIOR OUTSIDE THE GARDEN

In this painting, the light from flickering torches can be seen as coming from behind the Savior, acting as a foreshadowing. Judas raises his hand and touches Jesus, but the Savior doesn't return the gesture. John is looking back in disgust at the group that is coming toward them. John has seemingly just asked Judas, "What are you doing? You are intruding. Jesus is a holy man, not a criminal." Jesus is very calm, with a regal posture. He has just partaken of the "bitter cup" in the Garden of Gethsemane, and he is ready to face what lies ahead, knowing Judas' betrayal is part of the eternal plan.

JESUS STANDS BEFORE PILATE

John stays as close to Jesus as he can throughout this final night, watching what is happening, but he keeps being barred by the Roman guards. In this scene, John is as close to the Savior as he possibly can be, to the point that the guard's spear is actually stabbing into John's shoulder. Jesus is positioned below Caesar Augustus, and also below the statue of Caesar, symbolizing the brief power this earthly kingdom held over the King of Kings. Following that same idea, the door on the right side of the painting symbolizes the brief power of the Roman Empire, which will close within a few centuries, while the Savior's kingdom will go on forever. The Savior is framed by the guard's arm and spear, isolating him from the rest of the people in the painting and symbolizing that he would complete his mission alone. The back courts and open areas of the palace give a feeling of grandeur and a trust in worldly things, while the Savior of the World stands as a solitary figure.

CHRIST IS SCOURGED, SMITTEN

I desired to show John's anguish over the Savior's scourging, rather than show the scourging itself. This scene occurs right after the scourging has been completed. The rope that held the Savior's hands during the scourging has been cut, showing that John stayed through the entire ordeal. The guard at the entryway is aloof and uncaring about what is happening. This is a daily chore for him, so he rests on his spear, not really worried about John. Meanwhile, John's posture mirrors his feelings. His right arm clutches his clothes in frustration, but his left arm hangs loose, as if there is nothing more he can do. Near John's feet is a clipping from a thorn bush, accidentally dropped earlier by someone carrying the thorns that would become the Savior's crown of thorns.

CHRIST'S FINAL MOMENTS ON THE CROSS

I wanted to portray a view the Savior would have had during his final moments on the cross, with his eyes focused on the people he loved and who had supported him to the end. The Savior can also see Jerusalem in the background, whose inhabitants had forsaken him. Also in the background are the men who are waiting to remove the Savior's body from the cross. John is now gently comforting the Savior's mother Mary, as he had comforted the Savior. The two roads from Jerusalem frame the emotional group. They are all distraught, as if in shock, but John's expression is no longer filled with anger. He has come to a sad acceptance of what is happening, and he knows he has done everything he could for his Savior.

CHRIST'S BODY IS TAKEN TO THE TOMB

This scene at the tomb is filled with emotion. The women are grieving and preparing to leave, but John takes one last fleeting look at the Savior's body before it is taken into the unused tomb. I sought to portray the realism that the body was transported to the tomb in a mundane manner, carried there by mortal men. At this moment, John doesn't fully understand the concept of the resurrection. He has little comprehension that he will soon see the resurrected Savior, and feels this is the end of his ministry as a follower of the Savior. The right side of the painting shows a portion of the stone that will soon be rolled away when Christ is resurrected. In this scene, it is merely an overlooked piece of stone, but it would soon stand forever as the symbol of the Savior's empty tomb.

PETER AND JOHN SEE CHRIST'S BURIAL CLOTHES

When Peter and John heard the news that the tomb was empty, they both ran to the tomb. John reached the tomb first, but Peter was the first to enter it. In this scene, I chose to focus on the two apostles, rather than the discarded clothing. Peter is reaching out, almost in disbelief that these could actually be the clothes of the Savior. I particularly concentrated on Peter's hands. They are the strong, worn hands of a fisherman. I also see Peter's gesture to be symbolic of reaching out to take the mantle of the Church upon himself. John's expression is filled with the worry and despair of the previous three days. There is also a hint of wonder and astonishment, unsure whether the body has been taken by thieves, or if the Savior has indeed been resurrected.

CHRIST APPEARS TO HIS APOSTLES AT THE SEA OF TIBERIUS

While the apostles are in the forefront of the painting, the Savior is the true focal point. He has just taken off his headpiece, and has put out his hand to the apostles, beckoning to them. The apostles are still holding their nets, but they are focused on the Savior. Peter has recognized the Savior and he is poised to drop his net and dive into the sea to reach the Savior. John is still at the point of uncertainty, still holding firmly to the net. He is squinting his eyes as if to say, "Could it be? Is that Jesus?" The scene is set in the morning, symbolizing a new dawn, along with a new beginning for Christianity.

THE SAVIOR HAS PROMISED TO COME AGAIN IN GLORY

In this view of John writing the Book of Revelation, I chose to focus on the power of God coming down, rather than on the plagues and horrors that the book contains. John is on the seashore, as part of his exile on the Isle of Patmos. John can hear the roar of the sea as he writes, and the angels at the Savior's side are symbolic of a wave of glory coming to sweep away wickedness and fill the earth with righteousness. John finally seems at peace. His eyes are closed, symbolizing the direct revelation he is receiving from the Lord. There is also a hint of a storm in the background, because for some people the Second Coming will indeed be stormy. But the message of the painting is that Jesus Christ will bring salvation and eternal life to those who seek it.